388.042023
cc

Real

PASSENGER TRANSPO

REAL LIFE GUIDES

Practical guides for practical people

In this increasingly sophisticated world the need for manually skilled people to build our homes, cut our hair, fix our boilers and to make our cars go is greater than ever. As things progress, so the level of training and competence required of our skilled manual workers increases.

In this series of career guides from Trotman, we look in detail at what it takes to train for, get into, and be successful at a wide spectrum of practical careers. The *Real Life Guides* aim to inform and inspire young people and adults alike by providing comprehensive yet hard-hitting and often blunt information about what it takes to succeed in these careers.

Other titles in the series are:

Real Life Guide: The Armed Forces
Real Life Guide: The Beauty Industry
Real Life Guide: Carpentry and Cabinet-Making
Real Life Guide: Catering
Real Life Guide: Construction
Real Life Guide: Distribution and Logistics
Real Life Guide: Electrician
Real Life Guide: The Fire Service
Real Life Guide: Hairdressing
Real Life Guide: The Motor Industry
Real Life Guide: The Police Force
Real Life Guide: Plumbing
Real Life Guide: Retailing
Real Life Guide: Transport
Real Life Guide: Working Outdoors
Real Life Guide: Working with Animals and Wildlife
Real Life Guide: Working with Young People

trotman

Real Life GUIDES

PASSENGER TRANSPORT

WITHDRAWN

Bob Lees

Real Life Guide to Passenger Transport
This first edition published in 2006 by Trotman and Company Ltd
2 The Green, Richmond, Surrey TW9 1PL

© Trotman and Company Limited 2006

Editorial and Publishing Team
Author Bob Lees
Editorial Mina Patria, Editorial Director; Jo Jacomb, Editorial
Manager; Catherine Travers, Managing Editor; Ian Turner,
Editorial Assistant
Production Ken Ruskin, Head of Manufacturing and
Logistics
Sales and Marketing Suzanne Johnson, Marketing
Manager
Advertising Tom Lee, Commercial Director

Designed by XAB

British Library Cataloguing in Publication Data
A catalogue record for this book is available from the British
Library

ISBN 978 1 84455 109 ⁄

Typeset by Photoprint, Torquay
Printed and bound by Creative Print & Design, Wales

Real
Life
GUIDES

CONTENTS

About the author

Bob Lees was Principal of railway training schools in East Africa and Lecturer in Transport and Business Studies in Liverpool. For many years he lived in Central Africa where he was managing director of African subsidiaries of British international companies, including Lonrho (manufacturing, retail, wholesale and farming) and BOC (engineering, manufacturing and medical). He has undertaken consultancy/training assignments for the UN and prepared reports for submission to governments and international organisations such as the EEC and EIB.

As a careers writer he has written many of the books in the 'Working in ...' series and is a regular contributor to the Connexions Jobs4U website covering a wide range of subjects. He has also developed a distance learning programme for Africa.

Acknowledgements

The author would like to thank David Summers, Careers Manager at GoSkills, the Sector Skills Council for Passenger Transport for support and guidance in writing this book and Josie Campbell of Camlee Associates for research and assistance.

Introduction

AN EVERYDAY REALITY

Passenger transport is part of our everyday lives. You may go to school or work by bus, taxi or train. You probably use passenger transport to go shopping or to the cinema, and certainly when you go abroad on holiday by air or sea. You might also use a coach or train to reach a holiday resort in the UK. Even people who drive their own cars often use passenger transport in one form or another – it is usually easier to travel to places like central London by public transport than by car. People are continuously on the move using road, rail, air, sea or canal and this book looks in some detail at all of these means of transport, the jobs they provide and the type of people who do them.

Over 1.3 million people are engaged in the passenger transport industry, of whom over 500,000 are drivers of trains, buses and coaches.

A VAST RANGE OF OPPORTUNITY

Passenger transport offers a variety of work unheard of in any other sector, and employs large numbers of people at all levels. According to the Department for Transport, over 1.3 million people are engaged in the passenger transport industry, of whom over 500,000 are drivers of trains, buses and coaches. Those at the sharp end of the industry who come face-to-face with their customers include:

- Railway station staff
- Passenger service representatives
- Revenue collection staff
- Buffet car attendants
- Bus and coach drivers
- Tour guides
- Airline sales and check-in staff.

Behind the scenes you will find:

- Airline pilots
- Cabin crew
- Baggage handlers
- Train drivers
- Schedulers
- Control staff.

All these positions are supported by a mass of clerical and administrative personnel who, together with engineers, technicians and mechanics, keep vehicles and aircraft moving.

A POLITICAL TARGET

Transport is so important to the economy that it is strictly regulated by governments. They pass laws to ensure that users are given a fair service, and appoint regulatory bodies and associations to oversee safety procedures. There are also professional institutions such as The Chartered Institute of Logistics and Transport, whose membership is devoted to maintaining and improving standards within the profession, and Sector Skills Councils, such as GoSkills. These represent employers, and are an authority on recruitment, retention and skills shortages. They offer information on a

range of training courses, from NVQ1 through to degree level
and beyond.

Because of its strategic importance, transport is always in
the political arena. It has been a target for legislators and
environmentalists from the days of stagecoaches and the
early steam trains, which had to travel at walking pace
behind a man with a red flag. It has produced tremendous
problems, such as our congested roads and investment-
starved railways, but it has always been a focus for
innovation on a grand scale – just think of Eurostar and
Concorde!

A HUGE COMMUNITY

A unique feature about transport is that the people working
in it feel they are part of a huge community. This is probably
because they often have to work nights, shifts or on public
holidays, when most other people are at home. Also, many
of the jobs require a degree of interdependence rarely seen
elsewhere: airline pilots landing at a fogbound airport depend
on the air traffic controllers, and drivers of fast trains are
entirely dependent upon signallers. This nurtures a sense of
bonding across the whole industry.

If you want to become part of this huge family and find a job
in any area of passenger transport, this book will set out
your options. You will find information about the subject in
general, the array of jobs available and the levels at which
you can start. It will show you the qualifications you need to
achieve and suggest ways of getting them. It will also offer
advice and guidance on promotion prospects and it will tell
you what the jobs are really like – with no holds barred!

LEO JONES

Case study 1

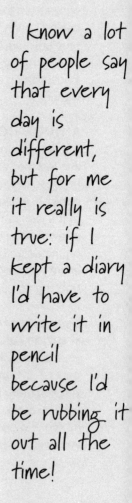

A SUCCESS STORY

Leo Jones may be only 25 years old, but his career is already flying along at Mach 3. As passenger operations manager at easyJet, Leo is known to millions of television viewers as one of the featured characters in the long-running series Airline. *He started working with the company only six years ago, but now runs a department of nearly 300 staff.*

How did you get into the aviation industry?
After studying Leisure and Tourism at college, I started by doing work experience for Britannia Airways, then moved into a check-in post with easyJet. My first attempt at promotion was screened on the first *Airline* series – when I was turned down for a supervisor's post!

What does your current job involve?
It's my job to run the easyJet operation in the airport, making sure that passengers get on the right plane at the right time, safely, securely and happily.

How many flights a day do you handle?
An average of 63 flights every shift, but occasionally things don't go smoothly. Delays and disruptions can occur

I know a lot of people say that every day is different, but for me it really is true: if I kept a diary I'd have to write it in pencil because I'd be rubbing it out all the time!

completely unannounced. Today, for instance, there's a strike in French airports, so we have dozens of passengers needing to rearrange their travel plans. Last week the runway was closed, which caused delays and all sorts of knock-on effects.

Do you have busy times of year?
Luton is a 24-hour airport – 8 million people a year come through our doors – and it gets even busier at peak holiday times in the summer and during the run-up to Christmas.

How much of your time is office-based?
Only about 15% of my day is in the office, but that's the way I like it. Most of my time is spent dealing with passengers and all the various airport departments, including check-in staff, gate staff and the aircraft dispatchers. The issues I have to deal with are rarely confined to the office and lots of practical solutions have to be found.

What sort of passenger issues do you deal with?
Although 99.9% of our passengers enjoy travelling with easyJet, one or two do make life a bit more difficult at times! I remember one man, who'd had too much to drink, didn't have a passport and had no idea where he was going. Eventually we put him up in a hotel for the night, as we have a zero-tolerance policy towards people who are not fit to fly.

What about the passengers we see complaining on the television when they are five minutes late for check-in and get turned away?
Don't forget that the passengers you see on television are always the ones with the most interesting complaints! People

can get very upset when they're travelling, particularly when they are late – after all, they are tired and stressed. Often, discussions that last for an hour are edited down to three minutes, and it's not always clear what lies behind our refusal to let people board planes late. We only have a 25-minute turnaround for flights and we have to submit accurate passenger figures so that the aircraft is fuelled correctly before it's allowed to take off. Delaying an aircraft by just a few minutes can have a knock-on effect and it's not fair on other passengers, so we have to be strict. It's much more technical than people imagine.

Do you use a lot of technology in your job?
Yes, because easyJet is a ticketless airline with a very high-tech passenger system – people can check in from home via the internet. In my job I use computers all the time, from monitoring statistics through to financial reporting.

What do you like about working in the aviation industry?
What I enjoy the most is the opportunity I've had to become such a generalist. I've learnt so much about all sorts of areas, not just operational ones. Five years ago I wouldn't even have recognised a profit and loss account, but now I feel completely comfortable with the financial side of things. I also have to deal with a lot of human resources issues, including performance management and training. I know a lot of people say that every day is different, but for me it really is true: if I kept a diary I'd have to write it in pencil because I'd be rubbing it out all the time!

What are the disadvantages?
My hours can be long, and working in a busy airport all day can be stressful. However I take regular exercise.

What is the future for budget airlines?
We work very differently from many other airlines, but it's an increasingly competitive market with many new airlines entering the scene. But the easyJet brand is very recognisable and well known now, and I'd like to think it's appreciated for maintaining high standards of safety and customer service as much as for being low-cost!

What's next for your career?
The transport industry is an international one so the world is truly my oyster. I've only been in this job a year, but I would like to spend some time overseas in the future.

What's the story?

With passenger transport being such a wide-ranging industry, this chapter aims to give you a brief overview of its four principal areas: road, rail, air and sea. Many of the companies will sound familiar, but a summary of what they do may help you decide if any of them appeals to you personally.

ROAD TRANSPORT

BUSES
Buses are the principal means of transportation in most towns, cities and rural areas. Although they operate as separate companies in their own area, many of them are owned by one of the larger transport groups such as Stagecoach, First, GoAhead, National Express or Arriva. In London, the vast majority of local bus services are private sector operations under contract to Transport for London. Smaller private companies tend to operate specialist services on routes not covered by the larger companies, often at times of peak demand, for shopping purposes or for older or disabled people.

COACHES
Coach services are operated across the country by National Express and in selected areas by Green Line, Scottish

Citylink and UlsterBus. The National Express Group plc are a leading international public transport group that carries more than 1 billion passengers a year worldwide on its bus, train, light rail and express coach operations. Luxury tourist coaches are operated by companies such as W A Shearings, who have also expanded their range to include holidays and hotel breaks. Local coach companies exist for hire, and are sometimes used for local journeys. Local councils often hire coaches to take children to and from school, or on school outings.

COMMUNITY TRANSPORT

The community transport sector is vast. Over 100,000 minibuses serving over 10 million passengers every year are used by voluntary and community groups, schools, colleges and local authorities, or to provide a door-to-door service for people who are unable to use other public transport.

Community bus permits are issued by the Traffic Commissioner to groups who want to run a local bus service on a voluntary, non-profit basis, using unpaid volunteer drivers. These groups are usually committees of volunteers sponsored by their local authority in places where there is no other bus service for the community in question. The Traffic Commissioner can, at his discretion, allow the operator to use the vehicle for non-local services (eg contract hire) that give financial backing to the local operation.

Community bus operators have to run their local services just as reliably as professional operators. The Traffic Commissioner must be satisfied that their maintenance facilities or arrangements are good enough. He can revoke the permit if standards are not kept up.

Over 100,000 minibuses serving over 10 million passengers every year are used by voluntary and community groups, schools, colleges and local authorities, or to provide a door-to-door service for people who are unable to use other public transport.

TAXIS AND PRIVATE HIRE VEHICLES

Taxis and private hire vehicles are available everywhere for people who are in a hurry or who want the convenience of personal transport. Although superficially they may seem to be identical there is a subtle difference. Taxis 'ply for hire' – they can be hailed in the street, be found at a taxi rank or be pre-booked, and are also known as 'black cabs' or 'hackney carriages'. The majority of taxis are licensed to carry five passengers, and they must all carry a roof sign with the word 'TAXI' clearly displayed. They have a red identification number displayed on a rear-mounted plate and in a prominent place in the interior.

DID YOU KNOW?

There are more than 150,000 taxi drivers or chauffeurs in the UK.

Private hire vehicles, on the other hand, can only be booked in advance through a licensed private hire operator. They are not allowed to pick up passengers in the street or from a rank. A journey is usually pre-booked by telephone or by visiting an operator's office in person. They must display a green identification number on a plate on the rear of the vehicle and in a prominent position in the interior. Private hire vehicles may be minicabs, ordinary cars, executive cars, limousines and chauffeur-driven cars. There are no restrictions on where they can work as long as they only take advance bookings.

The person who makes bookings for private hire vehicles is a private hire operator. Private hire operators are usually based at office premises in central areas and accept bookings over the telephone. Cars are dispatched to customers through the use of radios or computerised systems.

RAIL TRANSPORT

In 1994 British Rail was privatised and a number of private companies took over its responsibilities. Rail services are now provided by train operating companies (TOCs) under franchise agreements with the Strategic Rail Authority. Each company manages its rail services together with the majority of stations it uses. Network Rail, which is responsible for the track and line-side for the National Rail network (formerly Railtrack), is also responsible for the management of some of the largest rail stations.

THE TRAIN OPERATING COMPANIES (TOCS)

There are 27 train operating companies across the UK, including freight companies. Most of the present rail network radiates out from London to all corners of the country. The main routes between England, Scotland and Wales are operated by large companies such as GNER, First Great Western and Virgin, whilst smaller companies cover the more local routes such as the South West Trains, Southeastern and First TransPennine Express. In Scotland, the ScotRail franchise is operated by FirstGroup plc.

A complete list of companies and the areas in which they operate can be found in the Resources section.

EUROSTAR
London & Continental Railways (LCR) built and now operates the high-speed Channel Tunnel Rail Link (CTRL), and owns and operates the UK arm of the Eurostar international train service. It is the first major railway to have been constructed in the UK for over 100 years.

Eurostar is a unique rail travel business, spanning three countries with the best engineered, most advanced trains in the UK. Each year 15 million passengers use the cross-channel services of Eurostar from London (operating from London St Pancras International as of 2007) and Ashford to Paris, Brussels, Lille and Avignon, with connections throughout Europe. The high-speed lines have the capacity to accommodate six international trains per hour in each direction.

From 2007, St Pancras International will be Europe's largest passenger interchange. The Eurostar journey from there to Brussels will take only 1 hour 51 minutes, and to Paris 2 hours 15 minutes. The standard operating speed will be 186mph and it is envisaged that the link will eventually cater for 40 million passengers a year.

EUROTUNNEL PLC (UK)
Since 1994, Eurotunnel has been transporting people and goods through the Channel Tunnel between the UK and

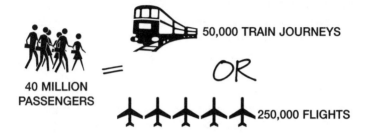

40 MILLION PASSENGERS = 50,000 TRAIN JOURNEYS *OR* 250,000 FLIGHTS

France. It operates a fleet of 25 shuttle trains, which carry cars, coaches and trucks. As a transport system, it is unequalled for speed, reliability and frequency. Eurotunnel manages the infrastructure of the Channel Tunnel and receives toll revenues from the train operating companies whose trains pass through it.

NETWORK RAIL

Network Rail oversees Britain's rail infrastructure. It owns and maintains 21,000 miles of track across Britain and its main customers are the train and freight operating companies who run the nation's train services. They provide access to the tracks for all passenger and freight trains.

Network Rail owns over 2500 stations throughout the UK. The majority of these are leased to, and managed by, the 27 train operating companies. However, 17 of the largest stations are managed by Network Rail itself.

DID YOU KNOW?

Network Rail owns some of the most impressive buildings in the country. Its estate is 57,000 hectares in size and comprises 97 light maintenance depots, over 11,250 line-side buildings and 755 maintenance delivery units.

Network Rail employs signallers and controllers to work on its lines, and station platform staff at the stations under its control. It has a workforce of over 30,000 employees engaged in track maintenance and replacement.

LONDON UNDERGROUND

The London underground system transports passengers between stations within Greater London, and its operation remains in the public sector through London Underground Ltd. In July 2003, Transport for London assumed managerial responsibility for London Underground. Carrying almost 1 billion passengers a year (almost half of all rail journeys in the country) the London Underground is a major railway company. It handles more passengers than any other individual railway company in the UK.

DID YOU KNOW?

Every day, nearly 3 million passengers travel on nearly 20,000 rail services.

GLASGOW UNDERGROUND

The Glasgow Underground operates one circular route in Glasgow, and is run by the Strathclyde Passenger Transport Executive.

TRAMS AND LIGHT RAILWAYS

These are again becoming a feature of our cities and towns. Before the Second World War most urban areas had tram services, some of which, such as in Leeds and Blackpool, became light railways as they reached into the suburbs. Liverpool had an overhead railway.

The major operators now are:

● Docklands Light Railway

- Nexus (Tyne & Wear Metro)
- Blackpool Trams
- Manchester Metrolink
- Stagecoach Supertram (Sheffield)
- West Midland Metro
- Croydon Tramlink
- Nottingham NET.

AIR TRANSPORT

THE CIVIL AVIATION AUTHORITY

The CAA is the UK's independent aviation regulator. It is an extremely varied organisation with many sub-groups, each of which is responsible for recruiting the people with the particular skills and knowledge that it requires. It includes:

The Directorate of Airspace Policy responsible for the planning and regulation of all UK airspace, including the navigation and communications infrastructure, which ensures safe and efficient operations.

The Consumer Protection Group regulates the finances and fitness of travel organisers, manages the Air Travel Organisers' Licensing (ATOL), licenses UK airlines and enforces European Council requirements.

The Economic Regulation Group regulates airports, air traffic services and airlines and provides advice on aviation policy from an economic standpoint.

The Safety Regulation Group ensures that UK civil aviation standards are set and achieved in a co-operative and cost-effective manner.

AIRPORTS

Airports are a key focus of modern life. Not only are they the arrival and departure points for domestic and international air travel, but increasingly they have become major centres for business and shopping, especially duty-free.

UK airports are found in the following locations:

- **London:** Gatwick, Heathrow, London City, Luton and Stansted
- **The Midlands:** Birmingham, Coventry, Nottingham East Midlands and Norwich
- **The North:** Blackpool, Doncaster, Humberside, Isle of Man, Leeds/Bradford, Liverpool, Manchester and Newcastle
- **Scotland:** Aberdeen, Dundee, Edinburgh, Glasgow, Inverness and Prestwick
- **The South:** Bournemouth, Bristol, Exeter and Southampton
- **Wales:** Cardiff and Swansea
- **Channel Islands:** Alderney, Guernsey and Jersey.

These airports are owned and operated by a variety of private and public bodies, sometimes with local authorities as shareholders. However, seven of them – London Heathrow, London Gatwick, London Stansted, Southampton, Glasgow, Edinburgh and Aberdeen – are owned and operated by BAA, a public company listed on the stock exchange.

On average 1700 aircraft arrive and depart from BAA airports every day – approximately 107 per hour of operation (one

On average 1700 aircraft arrive and depart from BAA airports every day — approximately 107 per hour of operation (one every 30 seconds). Over 700 destinations are served from them by around 300 airlines.

every 30 seconds). Over 700 destinations are served from them by around 300 airlines. The figures for all UK airports are an average of 2400 departures daily – approximately 160 per hour of operation, or one every 20 seconds!

Airport operators are spending more on new capacity than ever before, and investment in infrastructure at congested airports such as Heathrow and Stansted is set to continue. Spending on airport technologies such as air traffic control and security is also increasing, not only to meet the growing demand, but also by the need to reduce congestion and improve passenger throughput, safety and security.

AIRLINES
There are 23 major UK airlines, of which the largest are:

- British Airways
- BMI British Midland
- easyJet
- Virgin Atlantic.

Other major international airlines operating in and out of UK airports maintain offices and often a large staff presence at airports and in the major cities. These include the low-cost airline Ryanair and other major carriers from across the world. Ninety airlines are based at Heathrow and it is the world's busiest international airport. It is also the world's second busiest cargo port.

Major airlines operating out of Heathrow include British Airways, Virgin Atlantic, Air France, Alitalia, American Airlines, Cathay Pacific, Qantas, United Airlines, Thai Airways International, TAP Air Portugal, BMI British Midland, South African Airlines and Emirates Airline. Details of their head and regional offices, together with the areas in which they operate, can be found on their websites. This sector is very active and airlines come and go and change their names on a frequent basis.

Airlines are responsible for checking in passengers, baggage handling (from check-in through to delivery at the final destination), cargo, provision and fuelling of the aircraft, boarding of passengers (including those with special needs), passenger safety, and catering on board their aircraft. If an airline does not have a major presence at a particular airport, they may contract some of this work out to specialist operators and handling companies such as Servisair, Aviance and Inflight Cleaning Services.

SEA TRANSPORT

The development of air travel over the past 50 years has had a dramatic effect on sea transport. In the 1920s and 1930s, ocean liners were the main means of intercontinental travel. These great ships were floating showcases for the technology, architecture and art of the countries that built them. Competition to build the best and the fastest was immense, the coveted 'blue riband' being the reward for the fastest Atlantic crossing. They carried the rich and famous in mind-blowing luxury and, in less glamorous quarters, took many thousands of ordinary people to a new life in the New World.

The most famous ships of the Cunard fleet, operating a weekly express service across the Atlantic, were the *Mauretania*, *Lusitania*, *Aquitania*, *Queen Mary* and *Queen Elizabeth*. The first two made regular crossings to the USA during the First World War, during which the *Lusitania* was sunk. By the end of the Second World War in Europe the two 'Queens' had brought over 1 million troops to the war zone in Europe. The *Queen Elizabeth 2* was built after the Second World War (and saw service in the Falklands War) and now *Queen Mary 2* has been built as a cruise liner.

In the 1920s and 1930s, ocean liners were floating showcases for their nations' technology, architecture and art. They carried the rich and famous in mind-blowing luxury and, in less glamorous quarters, took many thousands of ordinary people to a new life in the New World.

The Peninsular and Orient Line (P&O) operated passenger and cargo-liner services to India, the Far East and Australia. The Orient Line originally operated passenger services to Australia, New Zealand and the Pacific coast of North America. At the outbreak of the Second World War, P&O

operated 2 million tons of shipping but over half of this was lost during the hostilities (182 ships in all).

The Union Castle Line operated passenger liners on round-Africa services from Southampton and London. The latest and most luxurious of these included the *Windsor Castle* and the *Transvaal Castle*.

Although by 1967 there was still a substantial fleet of British ocean liners and cross-channel packets, the age of the great transatlantic liners and the passenger and mail services to India, Australia and the Far East had ended. Purpose-built cruise ships and multi-purpose car ferries were beginning to appear and were to change the shape of passenger shipping.

THE MERCHANT NAVY

The Merchant Navy is the collective term for the British shipping industry. It includes companies operating everything from small tugs, coasters and ferries through to the large ocean-going tankers, bulk carriers, container and cruise ships operated by some of the most prestigious cruise companies.

The cruise sector of the shipping industry continues to grow, as the popularity of cruise holidays increases in line with the worldwide tourist trade. A large service-orientated crew is needed to look after the interests of passengers, who require quality catering, entertainment, accommodation and all the other facilities expected from a five-star 'floating' hotel.

3

KIMONE ENGLISH

Case study 2

THE RAILWAY TRAIN GUARD
*Kimone English works as a guard for
South West Trains Ltd. She's based at
Waterloo station in London, but spends
her time on trains heading out to places on
the suburban system such as Richmond,
Kingston and Clapham Junction.*

What does your job involve?
The safety of my train and passengers are
my main priority. I ensure that trains
depart at the right time, whilst delivering
excellent customer service. I patrol the
train regularly and make announcements
to passengers, telling them of any
changes to the booked route, delays and
revised times of arrival.

Is the work routine?
No two days are ever exactly the same on
the railway. My rota means I work different
routes and classes of trains on a daily
basis. I have to remain alert to deal with
problems and be ready to respond to
emergencies. This can involve anything
from route disruptions to assisting with a
broken-down train or dealing with sick,
drunk or unruly passengers.

I chose this work because I enjoy being outdoors, travelling and meeting different people.

What hours do you work?
I work a 42-hour week on shifts. My start time can be as
early as 4.20am and sometimes as late as 1am. If I finish
late and the trains have stopped running, I have to go home
on the bus, which takes twice as long! However, I benefit by
having a long weekend (Friday–Monday) once a month.

Do you have to carry a lot of equipment?
I am given an equipment bag, which contains items to be
used in emergency situations. These include a Bardic lamp
to attract a driver's attention at night or in bad weather. In
the daytime I use a green or a red flag. When I'm on or near
the tracks, I have to wear a high visibility vest, which ensures
I am visible to drivers. I am also issued with a mobile phone
and pager which give me direct contact with the signaller,
controller or British Transport Police if I ever need them. And
last but not least, I have a whistle to hurry passengers along!

What kind of training do you get?
Training is always ongoing, but when I joined I did an
intensive five-week guard course in Basingstoke. I am
trained in personnel track safety, so that I am fully competent
to protect the train I'm on as well as others in the event of
an emergency. Training is also given in disability awareness
and customer service.

How do you learn to deal with difficult passengers?
A lot of that boils down to experience, but one initiative
involves role-plays with a range of scenarios. We work with
actors posing as passengers so that we can get a better
understanding of how to deal with different situations. But I
find that most problems are diffused if I pass on the facts of
a situation to passengers. Once people have been informed

about the source of a problem, it's amazing how understanding they can be.

What kind of career progression can you expect?
After further training, I intend to become a guards manager or guards inspector. South West Trains offer opportunities to develop my skills further and they also offer a wide range of job choice should I decide to try something different – for instance I'm interested in working in the press office at some point. There is also an open learning centre on site which means I can further my education in my spare time.

What advice would you give to someone interested in becoming a guard?
I chose this work because I enjoy being outdoors, travelling and meeting different people. It's good to know that the excellent service I give to my passengers has a positive impact on their journey. It's important to be people-focused, with the ability to interact with people from different cultures. A pleasant attitude is a must and you should be able to live up to our values of giving the customers the best service possible.

4

What are the jobs?

Now that you've seen the variety of sectors on offer, it's time to take a look at the specifics. This chapter covers the sorts of qualifications that you'll need to embark on your chosen career.

WORKING ON THE ROADS

BUSES AND COACHES

There are now over 126,000 drivers and crew members employed on buses and coaches in the UK. As bus fleets have grown, staff numbers have increased. Operators employ large numbers of drivers with Passenger Carrying Vehicle (PCV) licenses, many of whom drive buses and act as conductors by selling tickets.

Drivers operate all kinds of vehicles. Whichever type of vehicle they drive, they need a driving licence that is appropriate to the category of vehicle. These are:

D1   **Minibuses**   vehicles between 9 and 16 passenger seats with a trailer up to 750 kg.

D1 & E   **Minibuses with trailer**   vehicles between 9 and 16 seats with trailer over 750 kg. The combination weight must not exceed 12000 kg and the weight

of the trailer must not exceed the unladen weight
of the towing vehicle.

D   **Buses**   any bus with more than 16 passenger
seats with a trailer up to 750 kg.

D & E   **Buses with trailer**   any bus with more than 16
passenger seats with a trailer over 750 kg.

The regulations for PCV licenses are very strict. Applicants
must already have a full EU driving licence and be at least
21 years old (or 18 years old to drive minibuses and on
certain bus routes). A PCV licence can be obtained at any
age over 21, providing applicants can pass the test and
meet the necessary medical, eyesight and health
requirements. Most bus and coach companies will take on
people with a driving licence and give them the necessary
training to acquire the PCV licence. PCV driver training
normally lasts for one to six weeks followed by a practical
and theoretical driving test and a medical examination.

Some drivers start as volunteers, driving community
transport, which they may combine with another role, for
example as a teacher or care assistant. To do this for non-
profit-making community organisations, they need to have
held a full EU driving licence for two years and to be at least
21 years old.

A Passenger Carrying Vehicle licence can be
obtained at any age over 21, providing applicants
can pass the test and meet the necessary
medical, eyesight and health requirements.

Inspectors are employed to carry out random checks en route and they in turn are supported by clerical and administrative staff. Most operators also have maintenance and repair depots staffed by engineers and mechanics.

Long distance and luxury coach operators employ drivers who may also be responsible for checking documentation of passengers, loading and unloading luggage and providing tourist information to passengers.

A new EU Directive means that from 10 September 2008 new Passenger Carrying Vehicle (PCV) drivers will also need to pass a Certificate of Professional Competence (CPC). The exact training and test requirements for the UK are not yet in place. Existing PCV drivers will be able to gain the CPC through periodic training. See the GoSkills website, listed in the Resources section, for more details.

Operator's licence   Every person intending to use a PCV on a road, for hire or reward, must apply to the Traffic Commissioner for an operator's licence. The role of traffic commissioners is to promote road safety and the safety of the travelling public.

Criminal records   Holders of a PCV operator's licence are required to report relevant convictions of themselves and those who work for them to the Traffic Commissioner. If they are applying for a minibus and/or bus licence, they must also tell the Traffic Commissioner about any other court convictions they have had – even if they are not to do with driving.

TAXIS AND PRIVATE HIRE

Drivers must hold a normal valid driving licence and ensure that the vehicle they are driving is properly licensed as a taxi or private hire vehicle. They will then be required to obtain a taxi driver's licence from the local authority in the area in which they operate. London taxi drivers are licensed by the Public Carriage Office. To get a licence, potential drivers must:

● Satisfy the licensing authority that they are fit and proper persons
● Pass criminal record checks
● Be over 21 years old
● Pass a geographical knowledge test of London streets
● Pass a medical
● Pass a driving test in a taxi.

Other authorities have similar regulations.

The Driving Standards Agency (DSA) have a test to examine the standard of taxi and private hire vehicle drivers called the Hackney Carriage Private Hire Test Assessment (HCPHTA). Some local councils include this as a licensing requirement.

CHAUFFEURS

For insurance reasons, chauffeurs must be over 21 years old. No qualifications except a driving licence are needed. Most employers demand a clean licence, but a few will consider applicants with three points. Some employers ask for an advanced driving certificate from the Institute of Advanced Motorists. Entrants also need several years' driving experience.

Most chauffeurs work for limousine companies. However, there are other openings with hotels, tour operators, car-hire companies, park and ride companies, business corporations and private individuals and families.

The British Chauffeurs Guild runs an employment agency specialising in vacancies for chauffeurs.

DRIVING INSTRUCTORS

Driving instructing is now big business and there is a shortage of instructors. There are around 37,000 Approved Driving Instructors (ADIs) and 7000 licensed trainee ADIs in the UK. There are also around 12,000 Probationary Driving Instructors (PDIs) attempting registration. A large proportion of these people are training individuals to pass tests for driving cars. Car driving instructors usually start work with a recognised driving school and then move on to become self-employed or franchisees. A franchisee pays a weekly fee to a driving school and in return is provided with a car and pupils.

> Car driving instructors usually start work with a recognised driving school and then move on to become self-employed or franchisees.

Many driving instructors provide training for bus and coach drivers – most large bus and coach operators train their own instructors. Others may work as specialists for large transport companies or tour operators. There is also a growing fleet trainer market.

Individuals starting training as driving instructors must first be registered with the Driving Standards Agency (DSA) as licensed trainees. The minimum age for registration is 21 years. A full UK, European Union (EU) or European Economic Area (EEA) driving licence should be held for at least three years, but applicants need at least four years' driving experience (it is possible to use a foreign licence, an automatic car driving licence or a provisional licence for the extra year's experience).

Before training, the applicant must be able to prove that they:

● Have held the appropriate licence/s for four out of the last six years
● Have not been disqualified from driving at any time in the last four years
● Are a suitable candidate for registration – all convictions, including motoring convictions are taken into account
● Have passed the ADI qualifying exam.

Due to these entry requirements for applicants, it is very rare to become an Approved Driving Instructor before the age of 23. Driving or teaching experience is advantageous. Some employers prefer their instructors to be over the age of 25, as this makes their insurance premiums lower.

There are three parts to the ADI qualifying exam:

Part One   a theory and hazard perception test performed on a computer touch screen. The pass mark for the multiple-choice theory test is 85%. Candidates must achieve 75% to pass the hazard perception test.

Part Two   the eyesight and driving ability test. Applicants have to demonstrate that they can read a new car number plate from 26.5 metres and an old car number plate from 27.5 metres. The driving ability test lasts for an hour and the trainee has to drive to an advanced standard, making no more than six errors.

Part Three   the practical/ability to teach test, which is split into two half-hour sessions. Trainees give the examiner two of the 12 pre-set driving lessons. In the first half hour they give the examiner a beginner-level lesson and in the second, an experienced-level lesson.

All the parts must be completed within two years.

Some applicants prepare for the exam independently, whilst others receive specialist training from ADI training establishments. The training is offered full time or part time via residential courses. Details are to found on training websites and if you want to find out more, either follow the major operators' links to their local companies or check your Yellow Pages. The website of GoSkills includes important and up-to-date information on training.

Due to the entry requirements for applicants, it is very rare to become an Approved Driving Instructor before the age of 23. Some employers prefer their instructors to be over 25 years old, as this makes their insurance premiums lower.

The Driving Instructors'Association (DIA) offers a Continuing Professional Development (CPD) programme to enable instructors to keep their training methods up to date.

ADMINISTRATION AND ENGINEERING

Whatever the size of the operation, from National Express to local bus operators, all road transport companies require administration staff and an engineering facility. Jobs in this sector include:

TRANSPORT MANAGER

Managers are employed by the larger passenger transport companies, travel and tourist companies, car fleet operators and courier services. They are responsible for planning, customer services, operations and fleet management, and often for engineering management. Managers are ultimately responsible for drafting policy, defining working conditions, providing services that people want, and making sure that government legislation is fully implemented.

Managers come from all types of background including those on graduate entry schemes and those who transfer in from completely different industries. They are normally required to experience work in every aspect of the industry during an initial training period of about 12–18 months.

TRANSPORT ADMINISTRATORS

It takes a small army to handle all the planning and support work for the bus and coach industry. Numeracy, literacy and organisation skills are required, and staff also need to be adaptable, as the tasks and challenges are often different every day. These may include:

- Helping to plan routes
- Conducting surveys
- Helping to organise timetables and routes
- Providing information
- Handling correspondence
- Managing money and preparing accounts
- Marketing and advertising.

Administrative staff also have many opportunities for training, possibly leading to an NVQ/SVQ. They will develop skills in typing/word processing and computing.

TRANSPORT SERVICE TECHNICIANS

Motor vehicle technicians maintain and repair cars, motorcycles, vans, lorries and other vehicles such as buses and coaches. Technicians work on a vehicle's engine, brakes, cooling system, steering, gearing and suspension. Today's vehicles are very sophisticated and include a lot of computerised and electronic systems; as a result, the work is now not simply mechanical but also requires skills with technology.

AUTO ELECTRICIAN

Auto electricians find and repair electrical faults in vehicles, and fit new electrical and electronic parts and accessories. In modern vehicles, electrical systems may include computer-controlled engine management systems, electronic ignition, digital display dashboards and electrically operated seats and windows. Auto electricians need to use a variety of testing equipment to find out what is wrong.

MOTOR VEHICLE BODY REPAIRER/REFINISHER/BUILDER

Motor vehicle body repairers, refinishers and builders repair

Today's vehicles are very sophisticated and include a lot of computerised and electronic systems; as a result, maintenance work is now not simply mechanical but also requires skills with technology.

damage caused by accidents or everyday wear and tear. They might do all the jobs involved, such as fitting, repairing or painting, or specialise in one part of the process.

TRANSPORT SCHEDULER
Transport schedulers ensure that buses leave the depot on time, properly staffed and equipped, and maintain the schedules according to the published timetables. Their activities may include preparing staff rotas to ensure the best use of drivers, and disciplining drivers in the event of a breach in company rules and regulations.

WORKING ON THE RAILWAYS
Forget the idea that train operating companies only employ train drivers and ticket collectors – they have around 3600 staff performing a huge range of roles. With them you could develop a career in anything from IT and finance to marketing and engineering. Railways employ drivers, customer operations leaders or guards, inspectors, clerical staff, engineering staff for maintenance and repairs of locomotives and coaches and an array of

DID YOU KNOW?

Current rail expansion means that more train drivers are needed, mostly along the mainline routes out of London and in the south of England.

administrative staff based mainly in their head offices around the country.

Whatever you do, you'll have the training you need to realise your full potential. Jobs can be divided into three categories:

- Customer facing
- Operations and track engineering
- Mechanical and electrical engineering.

CUSTOMER FACING
Customer facing on the railways provides a good entry point for people without specific qualifications. Experience counts here, and this can be obtained by starting at the bottom and working up the ladder. Job titles tend to differ from one rail company to another, but the following are general descriptions of the roles available:

- **Platform services staff** assist passengers and undertake duties on the platform such as cleaning and security. They must be aware of what is happening at all times
- **Train dispatchers** check that a train is ready to depart and signal to the driver to start
- **Station announcers** provide information to customers over the communications system
- **Clerical jobs at stations** include providing travel information and tickets, answering telephone enquiries, offering travel advice and handling money
- **Customer services managers** motivate and lead station staff in carrying out customer service duties and ensuring customer service and satisfaction
- **Station managers** have overall responsibility for staff and operations at larger stations

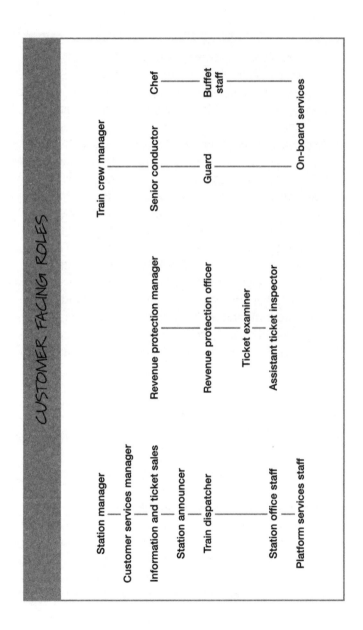

CUSTOMER FACING ROLES

Station manager

Customer services manager

Information and ticket sales

Station announcer

Train dispatcher

Station office staff

Platform services staff

Revenue protection manager

Revenue protection officer

Ticket examiner

Assistant ticket inspector

Train crew manager

Senior conductor

Guard

Chef

Buffet staff

On-board services

- **Revenue protection officers** or **ticket examiners** normally travel on trains checking the tickets of passengers in transit. They may be required to enforce payment or even eject passengers if tickets are not valid and further payment is refused. Considerable tact is necessary for this job
- **Assistant ticket inspectors** check tickets at the larger stations with manned barriers. They must be aware of the validity of all tickets presented by passengers
- **On-board services staff** include **guards** who ensure that the on-train environment is safe and comfortable. They make public announcements over the address system and keep customers informed; they sometimes walk through the carriages to check travel documents. **Stewards** operate trolley services, serve in the restaurant cars or buffet and **chefs** prepare and cook food
- **Train crew managers** supervise all on-board staff. They make sure that all company procedures are followed, solve on-board problems and manage cash, purchases and stock.

Customer-facing jobs on the railway provide a good entry point for young people and for people without specific qualifications.

OPERATIONS AND TRACK ENGINEERING

The **operating department** of a railway is concerned with the actual operation of the trains. Operating staff need to be quick on their feet, as even at the best of times – with good weather, clear track, and no mechanical problems – it can be stressful. Their job is to keep thousands of trains running

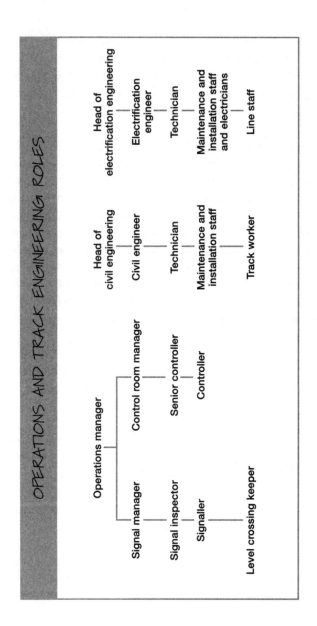

OPERATIONS AND TRACK ENGINEERING ROLES

on the network at any one time, to know where they are, where they're going next, and how to get them there on time. Good operations staff are accustomed to situations changing rapidly, and have to make appropriate decisions with maximum safety in mind at all times.

Train drivers of the latest express trains are the elite of the railway operating world. Their responsibilities are immense, driving at up to 150mph on a train weighing over 500 tonnes with up to 1000 passengers on board. Drivers are recruited and trained by the companies and generally must be over 21 years of age to be considered. Aptitude and personality tests precede training, followed by written and practical tests. Training may take up to a year. There are many different types of trains but drivers generally undertake the same type of training. They must be conversant with operating and signalling rules and regulations. The only way to progress to senior jobs in this area is by gaining experience.

DID YOU KNOW?

The first railway line to link two cities was built between Liverpool and Manchester.

Then there's the track – known as the 'Permanent Way'. This is maintained by a separate company named Network Rail. With train speeds now in excess of 150mph and set to increase, the standard of the track must be immaculate. It takes many hands and many skills to keep it that way. Technology and electrification also call upon a new set of skills, as do the demands for ever safer signalling.

Civil engineering work involves the track, bridges, tunnels and buildings. There are 2500 stations, 700 tunnels and 40,000 bridges on the British railway system and they all have to be looked after by civil engineers, technicians, maintenance staff and track workers. It's a massive engineering operation utilising a range of staff from general workers, apprentices and craftspeople to technicians, incorporated and chartered engineers.

Electrical engineers, technicians and **fitters** work on the installation and maintenance of overhead lines and on electrical equipment for locomotive power units.

Signal engineering utilises a similar range of electrical and electronic engineering staff including apprentices, electricians, technicians, and electrical and electronics engineers. **Signalling technicians** work on the installation and maintenance of the many different signalling systems used on the railways. These systems control the movement of trains in a safe and efficient manner and consist of integrated electronic control centres, panel signal boxes and manual lever frame boxes.

Signallers control the movement of trains via the operation of signals. Like the drivers, they work within rules and regulations to ensure a smooth and safe flow of traffic. They are responsible for a centralised control room for their particular section of track. The signalling systems include:

- Colour light signals that tell drivers when to stop, go or move slowly
- Systems controlling the points that switch trains from one track to another
- Circuits and track displays that inform signallers of train movements
- Systems to warn drivers or stop trains automatically if they pass a signal at danger.

Controllers work in a central control office. Their job is to control the signals operations in their area. They liaise with signallers, train operating companies, electricity suppliers and signal maintenance staff, checking the train movements on the control panel. Their job becomes stressful when problems and emergencies occur. Signallers are often promoted into this job, although there are more direct routes for qualified staff.

Rail track workers carry out the essential day-to-day inspection and maintenance of the Permanent Way. It involves checking for rail wear and faults, checking ballast and ensuring that the railway track is capable of carrying the high speed trains now being introduced. The job also includes replacement of track when necessary.

MECHANICAL AND ELECTRICAL ENGINEERING
It takes a lot of people to keep the trains running. Trains themselves need building and maintaining. **Electrical** and **mechanical engineering** involves a range of staff from apprentices, electricians, mechanics, fitters, technicians and electrical and mechanical engineers to maintain locomotives and rolling stock (carriages).

Details of recruitment and qualifications for all railway jobs appear in Chapter 6.

OTHER RAILWAY SYSTEMS
Eurostar and **Eurotunnel** employ the same range and type of staff as the train operating companies and Network Rail. There are plenty of career opportunities at Eurostar, from drivers and train managers who crew the trains to electricians, mechanics and engineers who work on them. It

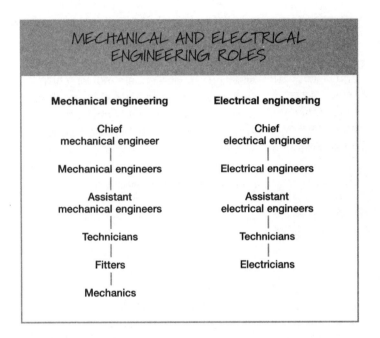

MECHANICAL AND ELECTRICAL
ENGINEERING ROLES

Mechanical engineering

Chief
mechanical engineer
|
Mechanical engineers
|
Assistant
mechanical engineers
|
Technicians
|
Fitters
|
Mechanics

Electrical engineering

Chief
electrical engineer
|
Electrical engineers
|
Assistant
electrical engineers
|
Technicians
|
Electricians

also employs customer services and sales staff in the UK, France and Belgium. Drivers, and many other staff, have to be able to speak French, and training courses are available for them. Eurotunnel employs over 3300 workers on track maintenance, signalling and civil engineering alone.

Light railways and **tram systems** have their own staffing and organisational structure. They all include customer facing and customer relations staff, administrative, engineering, operating and accounting personnel. A good example is the **Docklands Light Railway (DLR)**.

DLR trains are driven by an automatic system and do not require drivers. Each train is staffed by a **passenger service**

agent who is usually free to move around within the vehicle, overseeing safety, checking tickets, giving travel advice and assisting any passengers requiring help. Passenger service agents also close the doors when the central control system indicates that the train is ready to depart, first ensuring that it is safe to do so. They are also able to issue penalty fares on the spot to passengers without a valid ticket.

Although the railway is automatically operated, every passenger service agent is taught all aspects of train operation and can override the computer to drive manually, if and when necessary. Authority to drive manually is given by the controller in the control centre at Poplar, via the two-way radio that all passenger service agents carry. The passenger service agent reports any minor problems in a defect book which is handed in at the end of his/her shift. A vehicle health monitor, located on every train, is useful for diagnosing faults on board.

Passenger service managers travel around the system by train and car to assist where necessary and also carry out ticket inspections on the trains.

The **front line** and **control room staff** are backed up by various support teams who work around the clock to ensure that the day-to-day operations run smoothly. These include **engineering** and **maintenance staff**, who look after the trains, track and station facilities, such as lifts and ticket machines.

WORKING IN AVIATION

If you are employed in aviation you may work for an airline, either in the air or on the ground, or for one of the UK's 32 airports listed on page 16. The enormous range of jobs varies from cleaning the airport concourse to flying the largest intercontinental passenger aircraft, the Airbus A380.

In the air the jobs are **pilots** and **cabin crew**. They are employed by airlines flying into and out of the airport. Airline pilots fly aircraft on long- and short-haul flights. They are responsible for the safety of everyone on board. They usually work in a team of two with the senior pilot in charge of the aircraft.

On long-haul intercontinental flights aircraft usually carry two crews to ensure that suitable rest periods can be obtained. Both crews are usually on the flight deck for take-off and landing but during the flight they alternate responsibilities, one captain and one first officer retiring to separate rest areas for periods of up to five hours.

DID YOU KNOW?

UK airport departure numbers are expected to double by 2020.

Before joining the aircraft, pilots study the flight plan, altitude details and weather conditions. Before take-off they carry out

Retail shops are a big feature of any airport, especially in the duty-free area of international airports. They employ the usual range of managers and sales staff.

routine instrument checks and supervise refuelling and loading. During the flight they operate the controls, using computers to control and monitor the plane and keep in radio contact with air traffic controllers on the ground. From time-to-time they tell passengers about flight conditions and after landing they write a flight report.

Pilots spend long periods sitting on an enclosed flight deck with little chance of moving around. They work long, irregular hours and often spend nights away from home.

On the ground the jobs are more varied and include:

Air traffic controllers (ATCOs), who are needed at airports to issue instructions, advice and information to pilots. ATCOs may be:

- **Area controllers** responsible for a particular area of airspace keeping in constant radio contact with the pilots flying there
- **Approach controllers** who take over contact with pilots as they approach an airport and guide pilots while they land the aircraft. They sequence aircraft into safe approach patterns and link them to the guidance system for automatic landing when weather conditions are poor
- **Aerodrome controllers** who guide aircraft to parking stands after they land and to runways to ensure a safe take-off.

Ground services agents including **baggage handlers**, who have the most physically demanding job in the airport. Their main duties are:

- Baggage sorting
- Baggage security
- Aircraft loading/unloading
- Snow clearance
- Driving – baggage delivery to aircraft
- Operating specialised equipment.

This job involves far more than merely moving passengers' luggage. The baggage handling staff are the people who meet aircraft and marshal them onto the stands – positioning steps for disembarkation is the most physically challenging part of the job. They also need to know about operating machinery, technological equipment, storage logistics and transportation.

Customer service agents, whose main duties involve providing flight and tourist information to passengers when they request it. They may make public address announcements throughout the day and are usually responsible for coordinating ground transportation.

Fuel agents, who fuel the planes on the ground, usually on turnround when a variety of vehicles attend the aircraft to get it ready to depart.

Immigration officers and other immigration staff, who work for the Home Office and are civil servants.

Handling agents, who are responsible for recording passenger figures for a variety of purposes. They are often trained to work on the check-in desks. This involves labelling passengers' baggage for the correct flight, weighing baggage, allocating seats, checking identification and asking specific security questions.

Security officers, who work in one of the largest departments at any airport which is often supplemented by smaller specialist security organisations who report to the Security Manager.

Retail caterers, who employ chefs, porters, food servers, bartenders and duty managers who work in airport catering.

Aircraft caterers, who supply airlines with inflight meals. This is normally contracted out to specialist caterers who maintain premises close to major airports for food preparation and distribution.

Retail shops are a big feature of any airport, especially in the duty-free area of international airports. They employ the usual range of managers and sales staff.

Office staff work in the airport administration offices and range from clerical staff, IT operators, supervisors, HR staff and managers up to the level of airport manager.

Cleaning of the airport terminal and offices is often carried out by **contract staff** with experience of cleaning and using floor machines. Specialist cleaning services clean inside the aircraft.

Maintenance of mechanical and electrical services is usually carried out by contractors who employ people to service airport equipment as and when required. For example they are responsible for maintaining the ventilation systems (air handling unit) and the power supplied to aircraft on stand.

Bus drivers are employed to ferry passengers between the terminal and aircraft, and between terminals at large airports.

Aviation firefighters are stationed at all airports and are specially trained to fight aircraft fires and evacuate passengers.

And when you board your aircraft, fasten your seatbelt and wait for the engines to thrust you into the sky, don't forget the **engineers** and **technicians** who have checked and prepared those engines, and the airframes, to ensure that you do in fact take-off and land safely.

DID YOU KNOW?

The UK's aviation industry is big business — it is worth over £16 billion, employs over 200,000 people and handles more than 200 million passengers a year.

Commercial aircraft must be maintained to a very high standard, and teams of highly trained personnel are employed by the major airlines. Many airlines have their own **maintenance division** to carry out the regular servicing and repair of aircraft; training schemes and sponsorship schemes are available. The Royal Aeronautical Society (RAeS) website carries lists of employers.

Aircraft engineering jobs on airlines are mostly at technician level and include **aerospace engineering technicians** who use their mechanical, electrical or electronics skills to help build, maintain and repair aeroplanes and helicopters. They work as part of a team and might specialise in airframes, hydraulics, engines, fuel, pneumatics or avionics. In repair and maintenance, they carry out the regular servicing and repair of aircraft.

WORKING IN SHIPPING

The cruise ship industry depends upon a core of highly competent and professional British seafarers who are respected worldwide for their high standards, the quality of their training, their ability and their judgment. The jobs on a ship are:

The **master** or **captain** is the person in charge. He or she has full responsibility for the ship, the crew, the passengers, the safety of the ship and everyone on board, and for navigating the ship to where it needs to go.

The **chief engineer** is in charge of a ship's engineering and technical systems. This involves taking full responsibility for the operation and maintenance of a complex electrical and mechanical plant, and associated control systems.

Ship's officers have responsibility for a wide range of tasks, either in the deck, catering, purser or the engineering department. Officers control the work of ratings.

Ratings perform a wide range of technical and non-technical jobs, and have a lower level of responsibility.

Deck officers are responsible for controlling the navigation of the ship, communications, and ship stability.

Deck ratings assist in the navigation of the ship and are involved in operating deck machinery such as winches, and carrying out maintenance tasks.

Engineer officers are responsible for the provision and maintenance of all technical services on board, including the propulsion and auxiliary machinery in the engine room.

Engineer ratings are involved in routine maintenance, engine operation and machinery repair.

There are limited opportunities for entry as a rating. These are specifically with either the Royal Fleet Auxiliary, one of the British ferry companies such as P&O or Stena, or the numerous companies of the offshore support fleets.

Life on board a ship is a 24-hour-a-day operation, seven days a week, 52 weeks a year. The work is divided into shifts called watches, which are typically four hours on followed by eight hours off. At busy times this may increase to six hours on watch and six hours off.

There is no central recruiting agency and it is necessary to approach individual shipping companies or their agents to obtain a sponsored training opportunity. For a list of addresses and companies, see the Resources section.

Life on board a ship is a 24-hour-a-day operation, seven days a week, 52 weeks a year.

CATERING AND HOSPITALITY JOBS ON CRUISE LINERS
Cruise liners also require a large number of catering, entertainment and beauty staff. For experienced hospitality staff they can offer exciting career opportunities and the chance to visit exotic foreign locations. Competition for jobs is fierce, as thousands apply for limited places. To increase your chances of success you should:

● Apply for a specific position – general applications are not usually considered

- Keep your CV short and precise as large numbers of applications are received
- Speak and write good English. Other languages are only a bonus if your English is acceptable
- Do your homework first – find out about the cruise liner company before you apply
- Ensure you have a good health record.

For experienced hospitality staff, cruise liners can offer exciting career opportunities and the chance to visit exotic foreign locations.

Most companies prefer to take on people with hospitality experience, preferably in the role you are applying for, such as chef, silver service waiting or bar work.

Catering staff on cruise ships can expect to work 12 hours or more a day. You will be on a ship 24 hours a day, seven days a week – it's certainly not a holiday. Contracts typically last for six months, so make sure you are happy to be away from home for this period.

Tools of the trade

You've now seen what the jobs are, where they are and what they are like. Now it's decision time – you have to decide not only which area of passenger transport is for you, but what qualifications you have (or can get) to enable you to fulfil your potential.

THE GOOD NEWS
Let's start with the good news. Passenger transport probably offers better prospects for employment and promotion than almost any other industry. It offers employment at a basic level, for which formal qualifications are not required, through to the most demanding of the operational, engineering and management professions that require postgraduate education. There is something for everyone!

In the world of transport, a basic level of education means being able to read accurately, write legibly, undertake simple maths and exercise discipline. The rest can be learned on the job. Experience is valued very highly indeed and can lead to senior positions and top jobs.

THE NOT-SO-GOOD NEWS
In every profession or industry the triangle of promotion has a broad base, but in passenger transport it is broader than most. This means that you will be competing with many,

many other people for your first promotion. But don't lose heart. This is also one of its attractions, and the tens of thousands of jobs at the bottom of the triangle give way to thousands of well-paid and interesting positions on the way up the ladder, and this is where many people find their niche. These positions range from junior management and administrative jobs to senior operational posts, technicians and engineers. At the apex of the triangle, top management enjoys a status similar to that in any other comparable industry.

In the world of transport, a basic level of education means being able to read accurately, write legibly, undertake simple maths and exercise discipline. The rest can be learned on the job. Experience is valued very highly indeed and can lead to senior positions and top jobs.

COMMUNICATION SKILLS

Before looking at some of the specialist skills you have, or want to acquire, let's see how working in this sector may suit you. It almost goes without saying that in passenger transport the **ability to communicate** is vital. If you are customer facing – at the sharp end of the industry – you will have to be able to deal with customers of all types and in all situations. You may be selling them tickets, in person or on the telephone, or dealing with complaints. You may be in a position of responsibility such as a train conductor, bus inspector or aircrew having to deal with difficult passengers or travellers without the right ticket. In an emergency you may have to give instructions concisely and clearly: there will be no room for hesitation or timidity.

The ability to communicate clearly is just as important on the operational side of the business. Whether you are a pilot or an air traffic controller, there can be no room for error and you must be able to accept and give instructions clearly and concisely. On the engineering side, the ability to process and pass on information to operating units, sometimes at short notice, is essential.

DISCIPLINE AND SAFE WORKING

Although all our transport systems have excellent safety records, there is no room for complacency. **The ability to recognise and follow safe working practices** has to be learned and applied constantly. This is important for everyone in the industry, especially those involved with the movement of trains, road vehicles, aircraft and ships. Think of the **discipline and concentration** required by a railway signaller, the driver of a train or an air traffic controller, not just occasionally but **all the time**.

PRACTICAL SKILLS

Many of the jobs in passenger transport require practical skills, especially those relating to the engineering side of the business. Many also require **quick reactions** to daily situations, such as signal failures on the railways, bad weather on roads and operational delays to aircraft. You have to be decisive, able to think on your feet and adapt to constantly changing situations.

Training day

Let's begin by looking at the qualifications you may have. The chart on p. 56–57 will help you to work out how to put them to the most practical use.

Transport operators are well aware that the specialist nature of their industry places responsibility on them to train their employees for particular roles. As a result, if you are a new entrant to any of the jobs described here, you can expect to receive early specialised training before being allowed to take over full responsibility.

The transport industry works with government departments and agencies such as the DfES, and Sector Skills Councils such as GoSkills, to incorporate national training standards into their training programmes. It is possible to obtain vocational qualifications alongside experience, which may be relevant to other areas of work inside and outside the transport industry.

Formal apprenticeships are offered by the larger employers in England and Wales, graded as Apprenticeships (level 2) and Advanced Apprenticeships (level 3). **Graduates** may start out as trainee or assistant managers on a structured internal training scheme. GoSkills have full updated details of these on their website.

The sections that follow describe a selection of NVQs, BTECs, degrees and other qualifications available in the various sectors.

ROAD TRANSPORT

If you are working in road transport in a **clerical** or **driving**
capacity you can take relevant NVQs/SVQs in order to
progress. For example:

- Level 2 in Road Passenger Transport
- Levels 3, 4 and 5 in Transportation (only available as NVQ)
- Levels 2 and 3 in Traffic Office.

The Chartered Institute of Logistics and Transport (CILT) offer
Certificate, Diploma and Advanced Diploma qualifications,
which can be taken either part-time at a local college or by
distance learning. Colleges are listed on the CILT website
(see the Resources section).

Once in a job as a **bus** or **coach driver** you can take
examinations for SVQ/NVQ level 2 in Road Passenger
Transport. These are based on GoSkills standards and
specialise in bus, coach, community transport, passenger
support or customer service. You can progress to level 3 if
you work on longer coach tours which involve looking after
passengers overnight.

The Edexcel BTEC level 2 Certificate in Transporting
Passengers by Bus and Coach is a short programme
designed to support and enhance the knowledge of
prospective or existing drivers. It is suitable for new entrants,
for drivers who want to undertake continuing professional
development, or for drivers who want to update their
qualifications after an absence from driving.

Training varies between companies and may depend on your
past experience. It may be possible to work for an NVQ/SVQ

Qualification	Road	Rail	Air	Sea
NO FORMAL QUALIFICATIONS KEY SKILLS QUALIFICATIONS (ENGLAND AND WALES) CORE SKILLS (SCOTLAND)	Bus and coach driver Inspector Taxi driver PCV operator Vehicle dispatcher	Platform staff On-board services Buffet staff Guard Level crossing keeper Track worker Line staff	Security officer Retail caterer Bus driver Cleaner	Deck rating Waiter
GCSES (A–E) S GRADES (1–7) APPLIED GCSES	Trainee Entry to apprenticeships	Station announcer Dispatcher Clerical jobs Ticket examiner Entry to apprenticeships	Cabin crew Ground services agent Customer services agent Fuel agent Handling agent Firefighter	Cadet entry
AS (ADVANCED SUBSIDIARY) LEVELS APPLIED A LEVELS A LEVELS ADVANCED EXTENSION AWARDS (AEAS) ACCESS 1/2/3 INTERMEDIATE 1/2 SCOTTISH HIGHERS ADVANCED HIGHERS SCOTTISH GROUP AWARDS (SGAS)	Analyst IT operator Entry advanced apprenticeship Entry college courses Management trainee schemes Sales administration Traffic clerk Scheduler Traffic supervisor	Signaller Controller Customer services manager Station manager Entry to apprenticeships	Air traffic controller Office staff	Merchant Navy marine officer Merchant Navy deck officer Engineer rating Patrol officer (canal)

	(engineering/admin) Technician (engineering/account)	electrical and mechanical engineers	Engineering Technician	
NVQ/SVQ LEVEL 3/4 NVQ/SVQ LEVEL 5	Technician Transport management Driving instructor	Technician Signal manager Senior station manager Onboard chef and buffet staff	Electrical/electronic engineering Technician Accountant Senior office staff	Chef Craft specialist
BTEC NATIONAL AWARD/DIPLOMA/CERTIFICATE	Road transport engineer	Electronics and railway signals and telecommunication engineer	Accountant Administrator	Manager
BTEC (HNC), (HND) SQA (HNC), (HND)	Motor vehicle engineering	Railway engineer	Pilot Senior technician	Ship's officer
OTHER VOCATIONAL QUALIFICATIONS (EG CITY & GUILDS) PROFESSIONAL DEVELOPMENT AWARDS	Engineer Accountant	Railway engineer		Marine engineer Surveyor
DEGREE (BA, BSC, BENG ETC)	Transport manager Administration and business managers Transport planner	Operations manager Civil engineer Electrical engineer	Pilot/Senior Pilot Immigration officer Aerospace engineer	Marine engineer Captain
POSTGRADUATE DEGREE OR DIPLOMA	Fleet managers Chief accountant Financial manager Transport planner	Chief operations manager Chief Engineer	Senior airline manager	Senior manager

level 2 in Road Passenger Transport or Customer Service.
For **driver-conductors**, the BTEC level 2 Certificate in
Transporting Passengers by Bus and Coach, provided by
Edexcel, may also be suitable.

Most operators provide on-the-job training for new recruits.
The training generally lasts two to four weeks, and includes:

● Operating ticket machines
● Route familiarisation
● Customer care
● Health and safety matters.

For **driving instructors**, an NVQ/SVQ in Driving Instruction
at level 3 is suitable for all types of road vehicle.

RAIL TRANSPORT

Training to be a **railway train driver** takes up to a year and
is usually based in a company training centre. As well as
classroom sessions on safe working practices, rules and
regulations, and knowledge of train types, the training
includes practice in driving trains with a driver training
instructor, and learning routes by sitting alongside an
experienced driver. Trainees may also work towards an
NVQ/SVQ at level 2 in Rail Transport Operations (Driving).

There are no specific qualifications to start training as a
railway train driver. However, train operating companies do
look for a good standard of education, at least some
GCSEs/S grades or equivalent, preferably including English,
mathematics and a science or technical subject. They also
expect maturity and you need to be at least 21 years of age
before training can begin. However, young people aged 16

can start work at a station, and at 18 can work on board a train. In this way, they can gain knowledge of the railway system and experience in dealing with passengers before applying to become a trainee train driver.

There are no specific qualifications to start training as a railway train driver. However, train operating companies do look for a good standard of education, at least some GCSEs/S grades or equivalent, preferably including English, maths and a science or technical subject. They also expect maturity.

For **conductors** and **railway station assistants**, train operating companies look for people who have a good standard of spoken English and can deal confidently with money. The minimum age for these jobs is 18 years, and most companies favour mature people who have experience in other jobs.

All railway **signallers** undertake an initial full-time training course at a signalling school, which lasts nine weeks. Signallers generally start work in less complicated boxes and, with training and assessment, work their way into more complex signalling work.

DID YOU KNOW?

The imaginative yet stunningly simple route map of London Underground, recognised across the globe, was the brainchild of electrical draughtsman Harry Beck, who designed it back in 1933.

Civil, mechanical and electrical engineers, technicians and craftsmen and women play a vital role in the **railway engineering** aspect of the railway industry. Their skills and qualifications are sometimes obtained in other fields, but railways are increasingly seeking to recruit staff directly from schools, colleges and universities. They offer apprenticeships, graduate training, fast-track promotion schemes and internal courses to build up a core of talented home-grown technical staff.

AIR TRANSPORT
Airline cabin crew receive very careful selection and training which usually takes place in-house. Safety plays a large role in the curriculum for trainee crew members, who also learn about:

● Customer care
● First aid
● Report writing
● Pre- and post-flight checks
● Evacuating aircraft in an emergency
● Airline operation and sales.

Cabin crew are taught how to groom themselves correctly in terms of applying make-up, hair styling and maintaining a presentable uniform. Training is a mixture of theoretical and practical knowledge where much of the learning takes place in role-play situations.

There are numerous private organisations providing training for people wishing to become cabin crew, but the only nationally recognised qualifications are:

- Edexcel BTEC Certificate, Preparation for Air Cabin Crew Service – an introductory course
- EAL Intermediate Vocationally-Related Qualification in Air Cabin Crewing, awarded by EMTA Awards Ltd (EAL). This covers all aspects of the job and students are assessed on their performance in a mock-up air cabin
- NCFE level 2 certificate for Airline Cabin Crew.

There are a number S/NVQs based on GoSkills' standards. These include:

- Handling Air Passengers at level 2 and level 3
- Airside Ramp Services at level 2 and level 3, for baggage handlers and anyone providing ramp-side support in airports
- Controlling Airport Operations at levels 3 and 4, for anyone carrying out supervisory and management roles in airports.

Cabin crew are taught how to groom themselves correctly in terms of applying make-up, hair styling and maintaining a presentable uniform. Training is a mixture of theoretical and practical knowledge where much of the learning takes place in role-play situations.

Edexcel, EAL and NCFE have lists of approved colleges and training providers running these courses, some of which are approved by the Qualifications and Curriculum Authority.

DID YOU KNOW?

Work for airport baggage handlers is quite seasonal. There are often staff shortages.

Initial training for **air traffic controllers** – the National Air Traffic Services (NATS) – lasts between six and 18 months (including eight weeks' holiday) and is a mixture of study and practical training with students receiving 15 hours' flying training. Most of the courses are run at Hurn near Bournemouth. Examinations have to be passed at various stages to continue training and not everyone makes it through the process.

The college at Hurn has four high-tech computer simulators that can recreate real air traffic situations for practical training. Qualified instructors who have been controllers themselves teach in the classroom and in practical exercises. Successful trainees then go to an operational unit and work alongside an air traffic controller to gain practical training and a qualification. Licences must be gained from the Civil Aviation Authority (CAA) to practise, and these are validated by a period of supervised duty as a trainee air traffic controller.

Most **airline pilots** have to pay for their own training. Some airlines have sponsorship schemes, but the number of these has reduced considerably since 2001. Pilot training costs over £50,000, but under a sponsorship an airline would pay for all or part of it; after qualifying, you might have to repay the cost in instalments from your salary. Training begins at one of the residential pilot training schools approved by the Civil Aviation Authority.

Some airlines operate their own training schemes, which can take up to 18 months.

Most airline pilots have to pay for their own training. Some airlines have sponsorship schemes, but the number of these has reduced considerably since 2001. It is important to note that despite the cost of training there is no shortage of commercial pilots.

You start work as a co-pilot alongside a training captain on short-haul flights to give you maximum experience of take-off and landing. Eventually you become a fully qualified first officer.

It is important to note that despite the cost of training there is no shortage of commercial pilots.

SEA TRANSPORT
Deck ratings can work towards NVQ/SVQ level 2 in Marine Vessel Support, with options to train in deck or engineering, or the equivalent NVQ/SVQ in catering. Deck ratings also get the Efficient Deck Hand Certificate.

Trainees can apply to transfer to the apprenticeship for **officers** at any time. Marine apprenticeships lead to either the NVQ/SVQ level 3 Marine Vessel Operations or NVQ/SVQ level 3 in Marine Engineering Operations, together with the relevant certificates of competency for Officer of the Watch (OOW) status. Trainees for the **Royal Fleet Auxiliary** also take some Royal Navy training courses.

For **Officer Cadet Training** you can enter with at least four good GCSEs or SCEs in English, mathematics, physics or a combined science, with A levels or with Scottish Highers. For undergraduate entry you will need to meet the admission requirements of the universities/colleges offering the degree courses. For graduate entry, you will need to have a science-based degree.

7

SYED HAIDER

Case study 3

BUS DRIVER

Siyed Haider is a bus driver working for First Bradford. He has to drive in a city of steep hills leading up to windswept moors – and during rush hours make sure that he keeps to a strict timetable.

Why did you become a bus driver?
I was made redundant from a previous job so I applied for driver training with my present employer. After two months of training and a full medical examination I obtained my Passenger Carrying Vehicle (PCV) licence which means that I can drive buses and coaches carrying passengers.

Do you work shifts?
Of course. A typical day might start at 3am, which is the time some of the first buses leave the depot. I have to be there 15 minutes early to check my vehicle and I make sure that everything is in working order – the tyres, lights, doors and brakes. If there's a problem the bus has to be changed.

Do you always drive on the same route?
No, they vary. I drive the bus on selected routes keeping to the timetable as closely

I love the work and just wish that I had started earlier. I have lots of friends among the passengers and everyone at work is helpful.

as possible. This may be across the city centre to outlying areas, or on circular routes. This is difficult sometimes due to heavy traffic. I have to try to make up for any lost time without breaking the speed limit or upsetting the passengers.

Do you work alone?
Yes, usually. At bus stops I have to issue tickets from the machine installed on the bus, calculate the fare, give change and record passengers with passes. I have to check that everyone on the bus has a ticket. At the end of my shift I return to the depot, hand the bus back, record ticket closing numbers and check in the cash I have received.

What hours do you work?
I work a 38-hour week but the shifts vary enormously. Buses run in Bradford from 3am to midnight so I may work at any time between those hours. The shifts are spaced out to give me reasonable time off, and I have rest days.

Do you like the work?
I love the work and just wish that I had started earlier. I have lots of friends among the passengers and everyone at work is helpful.

What special skills and qualities are needed?
You must be prepared to work hard and concentrate all the time as a driver. You must also have a good sense of direction and the ability to relate to the needs of the passengers.

8

Transport planning

Transport planners make sure there is a safe, economical, reliable and environmentally friendly transport system working within a defined area. Their work may involve the following:

- Designing traffic management and calming schemes
- Studying road accidents and developing policies and schemes to reduce them
- Designing and implementing congestion charging and parking control schemes
- Designing car parks, road junctions or one-way traffic systems
- Deciding pedestrian priority and cycle route schemes
- Calculating the economics of major rail schemes
- Assessing the impact major new road and rail schemes will have on the environment
- Evaluating the effect of new airports on local transport systems
- Evaluating solutions to traffic problems
- Devising strategies for public consultation and involvement
- Preparing strategic transport plans for local authorities
- Writing transport assessments involving all forms of transport
- Helping teachers and parents to develop school travel plans.

DID YOU KNOW?

Not enough people are becoming transport planners. A total of around 900 new planners is needed each year.

Transport planners use simulation models to examine and manage travel demand and change travel behaviour, in line with government guidelines such as the reduction of car use. They recommend which area in a new development should be used for car parking, and they liaise and negotiate with different parties such as planning and highways authorities, resident groups, councillors, developers and transport providers.

Transport planners are usually experienced professionals from a wide range of disciplines and backgrounds, such as engineering, economics, town planning, urban design, mathematics, sociology, environmental science, geography or market research. The most common degree for entry is civil engineering, but a growing number of transport planners have obtained first degrees in transport, geography, mathematics, environmental studies or town planning with a transport option.

Transport planners are usually experienced professionals from a wide range of disciplines and backgrounds, but the most common degree for entry is civil engineering.

The transport planning profession is facing a serious skills shortage. It is estimated that there are approximately 10,000

planners active in the industry and there is a need for an
additional 500 planners every year. But retirement and career
changes account for the loss of 400 planners annually, so in
fact, the total number of new planners should be more like
900. Most people enter transport planning with a degree or
equivalent, although it is also possible to start work in a
planning department and obtain vocational qualifications.
These include NVQ/SVQ levels 3, 4 and 5 in Civil
Engineering or Transport Engineering/Planning. National
Certificates and Higher National Certificates (HNCs) in these
subjects are also available.

Transport law

If you are tempted to skip this brief chapter on the grounds that law is for lawyers, keep reading. Transport law affects you more than you think, and plays a significant part in most people's daily lives. For example if you walked over the road to the shop to buy this book, you were subject to traffic laws involving the conduct of pedestrians. If you drove to the nearest car park, you were subject to stringent road traffic laws, including those involving parking.

If you decide to work in transport at any level, you must be prepared to learn about the legal implications of your job — in particular, your obligations to your passengers or customers.

If you are reading this book as a customer on a bus, a train or an aircraft you are subject to the full extent of transport law as it applies to the carriage of passengers. You will have, or should have, a ticket which represents your contract with the bus or train company or airline (the carrier), and it will refer to Conditions of Carriage, a term which originated back in the nineteenth century. It is your responsibility to find out what they are and to comply with them.

At this stage it is not necessary for you to worry too much about the detail, but if you decide to work in transport at any level, you must be prepared to learn about the legal implications of your job – in particular, your obligations to your passengers or customers. These will vary according to the type of transport business you are in.

Transport of every kind has attracted the attention of regulators since the first passable road was built. The purpose has been to:

- Protect the operators
- Protect their customers
- Protect the public
- Control the operators.

In the early days, the operators themselves required protection from customers who expected unlimited liability from carriers for accidents or errors. So the earliest transport act was the original Carriers Act, drawn up in 1830, which forms the basis of modern transport law. It opened with:

> An Act for the more effectual Protection of Mail Contractors, Stage Coach Proprietors, and other Common Carriers for Hire, against the Loss of or Injury to Parcels or Packages delivered to them for Conveyance or Custody, the Value and Contents of which shall not be declared to them by the Owners thereof.

> Mail contractors, coach proprietors, and carriers not to be liable for loss of certain goods above the value of 10 shillings, unless they are delivered as such, and increased charge accepted.

This laid down the concept of limited liability for carriers that survives to this day, although the values have increased somewhat! Notice how it referred only to loss or injury to parcels and packages. It soon became clear, however, that customers also required protection from unscrupulous or careless operators, and successive acts and amendments aimed to remedy this.

Eventually it was impossible to make the slightest move on canals and railways that was not covered by an Act of Parliament. This regulation has continued through to the present day, as successive governments have attempted to improve relationships between carriers and customers. It has even extended to complete government control of operators in some instances, such as nationalisation of the railways and some road freight services. Some of the most important pieces of legislation have included:

- The Transport Act 1947 which nationalised the railways
- The Public Passenger Vehicles Act 1981 and the Transport Act 1985 – landmarks leading up to the Railways Act of 1993, which privatised the railways
- The Transport Act 2000 and the Railways Act of 2005, which provided for the Strategic Rail Authority (SRA) to be wound up and for its strategic and financial functions to pass to the Department for Transport.

Working in the passenger transport industry does not need detailed legal knowledge of this sort, but it does need an awareness of some of the legislation that concerns the particular industry in which you are employed. You also need to bear in mind that it is constantly changing. For example:

- Public Service Vehicle (PSV) drivers must ensure that they comply with the law regarding drivers' hours as laid down in the Road Transport (Working Time) Regulations 2005. Currently a driver must not drive for more than 10 hours a day or be on duty for more than 11 hours on any working day and there is a fine (currently up to £2500) for breach of these rules.

- The regulations also include tachograph rules (a tachograph is a device in a vehicle recording speed and travel time.) There is a fine (currently up to £5000) for failing to install or use a tachograph. Deliberate falsification of tachograph records can result in two years' imprisonment and/or a fine.

- New European Union legislation will require professional drivers of lorries of all sizes, and buses, coaches and minibuses to hold a Certificate of Professional Competence (CPC) as well as a driving licence.

- Passengers travelling by train must have tickets relating to their journey and are breaking the law if they do not have one. Railway staff responsible for the enforcement of this law may be ticket examiners, conductors or guards, who must know the extent of their powers when passengers are found without tickets or refuse to purchase one. They must also know how they stand in relation to other difficult situations, such as passengers becoming ill or violent.

> **DID YOU KNOW?**
>
> Passengers travelling by train must have tickets relating to their train journey and are breaking the law if they do not have one.

Similar problems are faced by maritime and airline workers, so be aware that transport is a highly regulated industry and is certain to remain so.

Making up your mind

Now you have to put the information contained in this book to the test. The range of jobs and areas of work may seem overwhelming, so you first have to decide whether a career in passenger transport is an attractive proposition. Some of its advantages were shown in the introduction – the interesting variety of jobs and the bonding that you get in an industry that never stops working, and where everyone depends upon everyone else. The answers to some of these frequently asked questions might help you to decide whether this is the world for you.

WHAT ABOUT JOB SECURITY?

A feature of the industry is that once you have qualified for a particular job, and are confirmed as being permanent, you will have reasonable job security provided you are efficient. Passenger transport is a stable industry, not too affected by the ups and downs of the economy. Also, the large organisations involved are usually able to absorb staff changes without resorting to redundancies.

However, some of the work is seasonal (such as baggage handling at tourist resort airports) and there are some specialised roles that are very competitive with no staff shortages, such as that of airline pilot.

WILL I HAVE TO WORK SHIFTS?

Not necessarily. There are large numbers of jobs that offer
a normal nine-to-five routine. However the really interesting
jobs are operational, and to do them you must be
prepared for some inconvenience in your personal life.
Buses, trains and aircraft don't wait for you to get out of
bed, and many of the jobs involve working shifts, including
some over weekends and bank holidays. But what's
wrong with that? Most people quickly adapt and enjoy the
freedom from the rush hour and days off when other
people are working.

HOW MUCH WILL I EARN?

This is a difficult one because of the wide range of jobs
available across the sector. With some notable and very
high-profile exceptions, such as Richard Branson, you will
never become a millionaire working in passenger transport.
Wages and salaries are usually based on national scales,
often tied in with trade union agreements. You will have a
reasonable basic salary, often supplemented by overtime
and shift allowances, and of course the opportunities for
promotion to more senior operational and management
positions are always available to ambitious people.

In general railway jobs are well paid, reflecting the
specialised and developing nature of the industry.

Reasonably up-to-date figures are always available on the
DfES Connexions website Jobs4U (www.connexions-
direct.com) together with very detailed descriptions of the
jobs themselves, qualifications and skills required for entry,
training and promotion prospects.

HOW QUICKLY CAN I EXPECT PROMOTION?

That depends on you and the job you are doing. Companies and organisations in this sector place great weight on a combination of experience and qualifications, not necessarily in that order. You must appreciate that acquiring both of these is your responsibility. Opportunities for study exist at every level, and most operators will encourage and help you to take advantage of them. However, only you can set this in motion and keep it going. In the same way, it is up to you to look around and ensure you explore all the avenues available to gain experience and promotion. Staying in the same job for ten years may provide you with an easy lifestyle, but it won't widen your experience or your horizons.

WHAT ABOUT HOLIDAYS?

Of course you will get holidays, and if you are lucky enough to work for an organisation that has a free ticket arrangement, you may be able to travel far and wide. However, you may find that these have to be taken at times that suit your employer. Airlines, for instance, are exceptionally busy at certain times of the year, so you may not find it easy to get away over Christmas, the New Year or during the summer holidays. Again this can be turned to your advantage – you can travel in comfort when other people are working.

WILL I BE ABLE TO MOVE BETWEEN THE DIFFERENT TRANSPORT OPERATORS?

Up to a point. Movement is certainly much easier now than it used to be. Much depends upon the type and level of job and the amount of specialisation you have. A railway signaller could not expect to be able to become an air traffic controller and if you become a Public Service Vehicle (PSV) driver you could not transfer to driving trains, but you could drive luxury coaches for another operator in a different environment. There are many similar areas of operation within companies where transfers could be made and, where they operate nationally, transfers to other parts of the country are possible. In fact they are good for experience and promotion prospects.

WILL THERE BE OPPORTUNITIES TO GO ABROAD?

Yes indeed. The skills you obtain working in passenger transport can be used anywhere in the world. If you work in aviation or the Merchant Navy, you may travel the world as part of your job and may be glad to get home occasionally. If you work on Eurostar or as a Public Service Vehicle (PSV) driver, you may travel throughout Europe. Transport is an international industry.

WHAT CAN I EXPECT TO GET OUT OF THE INDUSTRY PERSONALLY?

If you settle into the industry and begin to enjoy your work, you will get a sense of satisfaction at being part of the essential fabric of this country. Britain cannot function properly without an efficient internal transport system and the country is beginning to wake up to the realisation that some of our operations may be lagging behind other developed countries. This is apparent from the large number of new projects currently being undertaken, such as the new Eurostar terminal at St Pancras, the upgrading of north/south railway lines and services, new and extended airports, newly built luxury cruise liners and improved bus services. If you get immersed in all this you will eventually feel proud to be part of it. You will meet and work with a wide range of people who will have a challenging impact on your life, and in turn you will be better able to make your own contribution.

11

The last word

At this point you must admit that whatever else passenger transport may be, it is a long way from being a boring subject. This is partly because of its constantly changing patterns. A routine job in summer may change into a severe challenge in the winter months; a sudden emergency may close a packed airport for a whole day, requiring some very quick thinking on the part of the airport staff.

However, before you finally decide that this is the job for you, consider the following:

- The impact shift work will have on your health and social life
- That dealing with members of the public isn't always easy; verbal or even physical abuse does occur
- That you must learn how to deal with anti-social behaviour
- That public transport may not operate early or late enough to get you to and from work, so you may need your own transport
- That you will have to deal with all kinds of unexpected problems and you will need to exercise tact and diplomacy at all times.

You will need good customer service skills, which are more difficult to learn than driving skills! You will also have to develop good communication and leadership ability. Think of the responsibility that an airline stewardess has in the event of a crash landing, where she has to stand by the door and get everybody out as quickly as possible.

But the job has its compensations: days off when others are working; travelling around the country – or the world; and most of all, the cameradie that comes from working with like-minded professionals.

Passenger transport is a challenging job. Are you up to it?

	YES NO
I DON'T MIND WORKING EARLY, LATE AND NIGHT SHIFTS	☐ YES ☐ NO
I AM VERY GOOD AT TIMEKEEPING	☐ YES ☐ NO
I WOULD LIKE TO WORK OVERSEAS	☐ YES ☐ NO
I LOVE TRAVELLING AND MEETING PEOPLE	☐ YES ☐ NO
I WOULD LIKE A JOB WHERE I COULD WEAR A UNIFORM	☐ YES ☐ NO
I ENJOY WORKING OUTSIDE	☐ YES ☐ NO
I COULD NEVER WORK IN AN OFFICE	☐ YES ☐ NO
I THINK FIRST-RATE CUSTOMER SERVICE IS EXTREMELY IMPORTANT	☐ YES ☐ NO
I ENJOY BEING PART OF A TEAM	☐ YES ☐ NO
I THINK I AM A DISCIPLINED SORT OF PERSON	☐ YES ☐ NO

12

Resources

GENERAL

GOSKILLS

GoSkills is the Sector Skills Council for the passenger transport industry and its website contains a wealth of vital information, with many useful links to transport operating companies, government websites, employers and training providers.

Concorde House
Trinity Park
Solihull
West Midlands
B37 7UQ
T: 0121 635 5520
www.goskills.org

THE CHARTERED INSTITUTE OF LOGISTICS AND TRANSPORT (UK)

This is the professional body for individuals and organisations involved in the logistics and transport sectors. It offers examinations from CILT(UK) level 2 Introductory Certificate, to CILT(UK) Advanced Diploma in Transport, with the opportunity to continue studies for an MSc Passenger Transport Management or Logistics. It has two offices in the UK:

11–12 Buckingham Gate
London
SW1E 6LB
T: 01536 740104
www.iolt.org.uk

Logistics and Transport Centre
Earlstrees Court
Earlstrees Road
Corby
Northants
NN17 4AX
T: 01536 740100

INSTITUTE OF TRANSPORT ADMINISTRATION

The Institute welcomes members from all sectors of the
industry who have some involvement with administering
transport. In particular, it offers the opportunity for
membership to people who may not possess formal
academic or professional qualifications. Overseas
membership is available and the Institute is particularly active
in Hong Kong and West Africa.
The Mill House
11 Nightingale Road
Horsham
West Sussex
RH12 2NW
T: 01403 242412
www.iota.org.uk

CAREERS IN ROAD TRANSPORT

DRIVING STANDARDS AGENCY

The Driving Standards Agency is an executive agency of the
Department for Transport (DfT) and is part of the Driver,
Vehicle and Operator (DVO) group. Its aim is to promote
road safety through testing drivers, motorcyclists and driving
instructors fairly and efficiently, maintaining the registers of
Approved Driving Instructors (ADIs) and Large Goods Vehicle
Instructors, and supervising training for learner motorcyclists.

Stanley House
56 Talbot Street
Nottingham
NG1 5GU
T: 0115 901 2500
www.driving-tests.co.uk

DRIVER AND VEHICLE LICENSING AGENCY (DVLA)
Maintains registers of drivers and vehicles, and collects
vehicle excise duty (car tax).
Sandringham Park
Swansea
SA7 0EE
T: 0870 240 0009
www.dvla.gov.uk

DVLNI
Deals with driver and vehicle licensing in Northern Ireland.
County Hall
Castlerock Road
Coleraine
BT51 3TB
T: 028 704 1200
www.doeni.gov.uk/dvlni

DRIVING INSTRUCTORS' ASSOCIATION (DIA)
Safety House
Beddington Farm Road
Croydon
CR0 4XZ
T: 020 8665 5151
www.driving.org

**PRIVATE HIRE, HACKNEY CARRIAGE AND CHAUFFEUR
INDUSTRY TRAINING ORGANISATION**
Organises training courses for taxi drivers and operators in
conjunction with local authorities and local colleges.
c/o 14 Widdrington Terrace
North Shields
Tyne & Wear
NE29 0BZ
T/F: 0191 258 1955

BUS AND COACH OPERATORS

ARRIVA
One of the largest transport services organisations in
Europe.
www.arriva.co.uk

GO AHEAD
Has built up a significant share of the whole UK public
transport market, including bus and rail operating companies.
www.go-ahead.com

NATIONAL EXPRESS
The largest scheduled coach service provider in Europe.
Provides Britain's only scheduled coach network, reaching
around 1000 destinations in England, Scotland and Wales
and carrying more than 16 million passengers each year.
www.nationalexpress.com

STAGECOACH
Runs a fleet of around 7000 buses and coaches throughout
the UK.
www.stagecoachbus.co.uk

TRANSDEV
An international company providing tram systems, coaches, ski services and buses. Members of the group include London bus operators London United and London Sovereign, Bournemouth Transport Ltd (trading as Yellow Buses), and Blazefield Holdings in Harrogate.
www.transdevplc.co.uk

CAREERS ON THE RAILWAYS
For an interactive website containing factsheets, company details and careers information on all aspects of railway operation and employment, go to:
www.careersinrail.org

TRAIN OPERATING COMPANIES IN THE UK

TRAINS ONLINE
Provides TOC contact information, company reviews, a station information search with OS maps, aerial photos, TIPLOC codes and much more.
www.trainsonline.co.uk

ARRIVA TRAINS WALES
www.arrivatrainswales.co.uk

C2C
Provides rail services for London, Tilbury and Southend.
www.c2c-online.co.uk

CENTRAL TRAINS LTD
Provides local and long distance services across central England.
www.centraltrains.co.uk

CHILTERN RAILWAYS
Operates trains between London, Birmingham, High Wycombe and Aylesbury.
www.chilternrailways.co.uk

DOCKLANDS LIGHT RAILWAY
www.tfl.gov.uk

EUROSTAR
www.eurostar.com

FIRST CAPITAL CONNECT
Operates trains between London, Brighton, Bedford, Peterborough, Cambridge and King's Lynn.
www.firstcapitalconnect.co.uk

FIRST GREAT WESTERN
Runs train services between London Paddington, South Wales, the Cotswolds and the west of England.
www.firstgreatwestern.co.uk

FIRST SCOTRAIL
Operates rail services throughout Scotland plus the Caledonian Sleepers.
www.firstgroup.com/scotrail

FIRST TRANSPENNINE EXPRESS
Operates services between the west and east coasts in the north of England, including Manchester airport.
www.tpexpress.co.uk

GATWICK EXPRESS
The high-speed link between Gatwick Airport and London Victoria.
www.gatwickexpress.co.uk

GREAT NORTH EASTERN RAILWAY
Provides trains from London Kings Cross to the northeast of England and Scotland.
www.gner.co.uk

HEATHROW CONNECT
The direct rail link to Heathrow Airport from Paddington and five intermediate stations at 30-minute intervals.
www.heathrowconnect.com

HEATHROW EXPRESS
Heathrow to London Paddington in 15 minutes, every 15 minutes.
www.heathrowexpress.com

HULL TRAINS
Offers a direct London to Hull service.
www.hulltrains.co.uk

ISLAND LINE
Operates the passenger railway on the Isle of Wight, serving Ryde, Brading, Sandown, Lake and Shanklin.
www.island-line.co.uk

LONDON UNDERGROUND
www.tfl.gov.uk/tube

MERSEY RAIL
Operates 67 stations across Merseyside and the Wirral, including underground services.
www.merseyrail.org

MIDLAND MAINLINE
Operates from Yorkshire and the East Midlands to London St Pancras.
www.midlandmainline.com

NI RAILWAYS
Operates a coordinated service with the bus companies across Northern Ireland.
www.nirailways.co.uk

NORTHERN RAIL
Operates local and inter-regional services across the north and northeast of England.
www.northernrail.org

ONE RAILWAY
Operates services from London Liverpool Street to the east of England.
www.onerailway.com

SILVERLINK TRAIN SERVICES
Operates trains between London and Birmingham, as well as some suburban trains in London.
www.silverlink-trains.com

SOUTHERN RAILWAYS
Provides connections from London Victoria and London Bridge to the Kent coast and Portsmouth, Southampton and Bournemouth.
www.southernrailway.com

SOUTH EASTERN TRAINS
Provides services from Central London to mid-Kent,
Canterbury, Tunbridge Wells and the Kent coast at Deal and
Margate.
www.southeasternrailway.co.uk

SOUTH WEST TRAINS
Operates services from Waterloo to the southwest including
Portsmouth, Southampton, Exeter, Plymouth and
Penzance.
www.southwesttrains.co.uk

STANSTEAD EXPRESS
The shuttle service from London Liverpool Street station to
Stanstead Airport.
www.stanstedexpress.com

VIRGIN TRAINS
Operates mainly cross-country from Aberdeen to Penzance,
from Holyhead and Manchester to Euston and on to
Brighton.
www.virgintrains.co.uk

CAREERS IN AVIATION

THE BRITISH AIRLINE PILOTS' ASSOCIATION (BALPA)
With a membership of more than 8000, over 75% of Britain's
pilots and flight engineers belong to BALPA. The website
contains information on how to become a pilot.
81 New Road
Harlington

Hayes
Middlesex
UB3 5BG
T: 020 8476 4000
www.balpa.org

UK AIRLINES

AIR 2000
A low-cost UK charter airline serving Europe. Part of First
Choice.
www.air2000.com

ASTRAEUS
Independent charter airlines, flies to destinations throughout
Europe, Asia, the Middle East, North America and Africa.
www.flyastraeus.com

AURIGNY
Based in the Channel Islands. Provides scheduled services
between Guernsey, Jersey and Alderney, and to destinations
in the UK and Continental Europe.
www.aurigny.com

BAC EXPRESS
A leading force in the UK turboprop contract and charter
market.
www.bacexpress.com

BRITISH AIRWAYS
The UK's largest international scheduled airline.
www.britishairways.com

BRITISH MIDLAND (BMI)
The UK's second-largest full service airline.
www.flybmi.com

BRITISH NORTHWEST AIRLINES
Flies between Blackpool, the Isle of Man and Belfast.
www.flybnwa.co.uk

EASTERN AIRWAYS
Flies to 17 airports within the UK, and to the majority of
airports across Europe.
www.easternairways.com

EASYJET
Low-cost airline with operating bases throughout the UK and
mainland Europe.
www.easyjet.com

JET2.COM
Low-cost airline to major European destinations.
www.jet2.com

MONARCH AIRLINES
Runs both scheduled and chartered flights. Offers cheap
flights to popular European holiday destinations.
www.monarch-airlines.com

VIRGIN ATLANTIC AIRWAYS
Scheduled flights to all continents.
www.virgin-atlantic.co.uk

CAREERS IN SHIPPING

GO TO SEA
A web portal with links to useful shipping-related websites.
www.gotosea.org

MERCHANT NAVY TRAINING BOARD
Since its inception in 1937, the MNTB has existed as the shipping industry's body for developing and promoting the training and qualification of seafarers. Now it is the centre of expertise and information on careers, qualifications, training opportunities, training provision and skill needs, and issues in the industry.
12 Carthusian Street
London
EC1M 6EZ
T: 0800 085 0973
www.mntb.org.uk

CRUISE LINES

CUNARD LINE
Provides transatlantic crossings in the world's largest liner and cruises around the world.
www.cunard.co.uk

EASYCRUISE.COM
Runs budget cruises around the Mediterranean.
www.easycruise.com

FRED OLSEN CRUISE LINES
Provides worldwide cruises from the UK.
www.fredolsen.co.uk

P&O CRUISES
World cruise company based in Southampton.
www.pocruises.com

THOMSON CRUISES
Provides luxury cruising around Europe and the Canary Islands.
www.thomsonbeach.co.uk